THE GHOSTLY TALES OF

MILWAUKEE

For my favorite Spooky Americans:
Noah Maloney and Corey Lardinois

Published by Arcadia Children's Books
A Division of Arcadia Publishing
Charleston, SC
www.arcadiapublishing.com

Spooky America is a trademark of Arcadia Publishing, Inc.

First published 2021

Manufactured in the United States

ISBN 978-1-4671-9834-9

Library of Congress Control Number: 2021938350

Notice: The information in this book is true and complete to the best of our knowledge. It is offered without guarantee on the part of the author or Arcadia Publishing. The author and Arcadia Publishing disclaim all liability in connection with the use of this book.

Images courtesy of Shutterstock.com; pp. 2, 6, 48, 80 Anna Lardinois.

Spooky America

THE
GHOSTLY TALES
OF
MILWAUKEE

ANNA LARDINOIS

Adapted from *Milwaukee Ghosts and Legends*
by Anna Lardinois

arcadia
CHILDREN'S BOOKS

WISCONSIN

LAKE
MICHIGAN

MILWAUKEE

TABLE OF CONTENTS & MAP KEY

MICHIGAN

Introduction

Founded in 1846, Milwaukee is the largest city in Wisconsin. It has the state's tallest building (the forty-two floors of the US Bank building), the Bucks and the Brewers, the world-famous Milwaukee Art Museum, and of course, Summerfest! Every year, millions of people visit the city, some for work and many others to vacation in Brew City.

All of that is interesting, but this is a book about Milwaukee ghosts.

You might be thinking, "Wait! Milwaukee has ghosts?" It sure does. In fact, the city has far more ghostly tales than could fit into a single book. This collection of tales represents just a sliver of the spooky former Milwaukee residents whose spirits still linger on the streets of Brew City. In these pages, you'll meet some famous ghosts, tour a few haunted graveyards, and learn about the spooky side of some very well-known Milwaukee locations.

Are ghosts real? People have a lot of opinions on the subject. But no one has found a way to DEFINITELY prove whether or not ghosts really exist. You don't have to believe in ghosts to read this book. All of the stories inside are true, all of the people mentioned in the tales really lived, and all of the dates mentioned are historically accurate. Whether or not you believe in ghosts, you are sure to enjoy these creepy tales and learn a little bit more about Milwaukee while you're reading.

So, what do you think? Are the ghosts in this book real? Is Milwaukee a haunted city? The best way to find out is to read on and decide for yourself!

The Pabst Mansion

Superstar Specters: Milwaukee's Most Famous Ghosts

Milwaukee has its share of famous ghosts. From the baseball-loving Pfister Ghost to one of the city's favorite beer barons, some of Brew City's best-known citizens have decided to stick around town in spirit form.

Not all of the city's favorite ghosts were famous in their lifetimes. But they have been around for such a long time that they have become as well known as the places they continue to haunt.

Read on to meet a few of Milwaukee's most spook-tacular spirits.

Courting in the Caves

Have you ever heard someone call Milwaukee "Brew City?" Milwaukee got that nickname because it was the home of so many breweries in the city's early days. In 1855, a man named Frederick Miller opened Miller Brewery in the city. People loved his beer, and it soon became famous. It was so popular that it is still being brewed in Milwaukee today!

A long time ago, before refrigeration was invented, beer was stored in manmade underground caves to keep the freshly brewed beer cold. Miller Brewery had caves to store its beer, but after mechanical refrigeration was installed in the factory in 1897, it didn't need to use the caves anymore. Working in the brewery was a hot, sweaty job, especially in summertime. The cold, dark caves were the perfect place for workers to cool down after their workday was over. Today, people still visit the caves to see the history of the brewery, and sometimes those visitors catch an unexpected glimpse of two spirits who still linger in the shadows.

This famous story begins many summers ago at the turn of the century, when a young man who worked at the brewery began a romance with a girl who lived nearby. Each night when the young man ended his shift, he would meet the girl at the doorway that led to the mouth of the Miller Caves. Together, they would walk hand in hand through the cool, dark caves, their footsteps softly echoing

around them. They spent nearly every night that summer walking through the caves, talking, and occasionally sharing a kiss in the dark passageways. By the end of the summer, the pair were in love.

One night the girl waited for her sweetheart at the mouth of the cave, like she had done most nights that summer. As the minutes ticked by, her excitement about seeing the boy turned to concern when he did not arrive. She waited and waited, but he never came to meet her. Eventually she trudged home, heartbroken, because she believed he had rejected her.

With a heavy heart, the heartsick girl crawled into bed and pulled the covers over her head. She then fell into a deep sleep. Hours later, the girl awoke to frantic knocks on her bedroom door. As she sat up in bed, her mother burst into the room. Her mother told her that the reason the boy had not shown up for their date that night was because he was in an accident on his way to meet her.

As the boy had dashed to meet the girl, he slipped on the stone staircase in the cave and hit his head on the edge of a stair. He was unconscious when he was discovered and was quickly rushed to the doctor. His injury was severe, and little could be done for him. The boy never regained consciousness and died days later. The girl was overcome with grief over the death of the boy she loved. Each night, she would cry herself to sleep because she missed him so much. Within months, the girl was laid to rest in her own grave. The doctor said she died of a lung ailment, but those who knew her best believed she died of a broken heart.

The death of the young sweethearts was not the end of their story. Shortly after the girl was buried, people reported seeing a shimmering mist appear at the doorway of the brewery cave at nightfall. This curious glow sent shivers up the spines of all who saw it, and that was just the start of the supernatural activity. In the coming weeks, strange things started

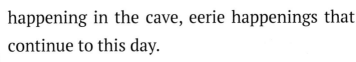

happening in the cave, eerie happenings that continue to this day.

Scores of security guards have claimed to hear the sounds of footsteps echoing in the darkened cave when no one is present. Witnesses have seen the shadows of two people pass along the cold stone walls of the cave, yet no earthly creature is in the cave. With shaking hands, the guards tell of the quiet laughter and snippets of conversations they hear coming from the lonely walkways late in the evening, long after everyone has left for the day. Try as they might to discover the source of these sounds, when security guards investigate, they always find themselves all alone in the darkness. Or are they?

Those who have experienced these spine-tingling occurrences believe it is the couple who fell in love in the caves so many summers ago, reunited after death in the place that meant the most to them. It is said this ghostly pair still spend their nights walking hand in hand through the cave, happy to spend eternity in each other's company. Perhaps you might be lucky enough to catch sight of the couple, destined to stay forever young, as you tour the underground caves at the Miller Brewery.

Captain Pabst and His Beautiful Mansion

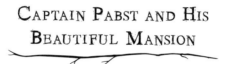

Frederick Pabst is one of Milwaukee's most well-known historical figures. He was born Johann Gottlieb Friedrich Pabst in Germany on March 28, 1836. When he was twelve years old, his family moved to the United States and began a new life in Chicago.

As a young boy, Frederick was a very hard worker, and by the time he was fourteen, he was employed as a cabin boy on a Great Lakes steamer ship. Young Frederick would collect tickets from the passengers on the ship, help out in the kitchen, and assist with any other jobs that needed to be done onboard. Little did those passengers know that the industrious boy swabbing the decks of the steamer would one day become one of the most famous beer makers in the history of Milwaukee—and one of its most famous ghosts!

Frederick never left a job undone, and he could always be counted on to go the extra mile and put forth his best efforts. After years of diligent work, he became a captain at the age of twenty-one. He was dedicated to working on Lake Michigan until Maria Best boarded his ship one day as a passenger. Frederick was smitten with the pretty daughter of the man who owned one of Milwaukee's largest breweries. Maria was flattered by the attention from the dashing young captain, and the couple soon began a romance. After a two-year courtship, Frederick and Maria married in 1862. It was decided he would stay on land and go to work for Maria's father at the Best & Co. Brewery.

Frederick toiled just as hard at the brewery as he did when he was a sailor. And within a few years, he took over the brewery and the company was renamed Pabst Brewery. All of this hard work made him a very rich man, and he felt it was time for his family to have a home that showed the world how prosperous he had become. He decided to build an elegant home for his family on the most exclusive street in the city. In 1890, he started construction of the building we now call the Pabst Mansion.

It took two years for the builders to construct the home. When they were done, the home had five floors and sixty-six rooms! Frederick and Maria filled their mansion with expensive art and furnishings from all over the world. The Pabst family loved their majestic new home.

But as time passed, Frederick's health began to suffer. He grew sicker, and in the final year of his life, he suffered a number of strokes. He died in the Pabst Mansion at age sixty-eight on New Year's Day 1904. The Pabst family held his funeral in the mansion's music room.

Today, people from all over the world come to visit the Pabst Mansion to see what life was like inside the exquisite home of this famous family. Some people are interested in the art on display in the mansion, and others are interested in the history of the structure, but there are a few who visit the Pabst Mansion in hopes of catching a glimpse of the elusive Captain Pabst himself!

After the home became a museum, people began to tell tales of strange happenings inside the mansion. Over the years, people have

witnessed the heavy, ornately carved, solid wood doors opening and closing on their own. Doors this heavy could not be moved without the help of someone—or something! What could it be? While walking through the house, people have reported feeling unexplained cold breezes and strange cold spots in the home. Might that be a sign the captain still lingers in his grand home?

A former volunteer at the museum remembers an evening in March years ago when they were busy preparing to welcome guests into the home. Taking a quick look around the room, one of the volunteers noticed that the unlit candles placed inside a glittering candelabra had fallen over. The volunteer quickly replaced the candles, giving them a bit of a twist to ensure they would stay in place. She then continued with her chores. When she turned around, she noticed the candles had, once again, fallen out of the candelabra!

The woman was puzzled. They had used this candelabra for years without any problems. Why wouldn't the candles stay in place that night? As she placed the candles back in the holder for a third time, she wondered if someone was playing a prank on her. She mentioned this strange happening to another volunteer, who pointed out that the date was March 28—Captain Pabst's birthday. Once the captain's birthday was acknowledged, the candles suddenly stopped falling out of their holders. Was this mischievous moving of the candles Captain Pabst's way of "blowing out" his birthday candles from beyond the grave?

It is not just volunteers at the museum who have unusual experiences in the building. The stories most often told are from frustrated tradespeople who do repairs or restoration work on the historic home. For years, many of those hired to work on house have been bothered by a man who is overly interested in their work. The mysterious man is described as older, with a full mustache and prominent goatee. He will hover over the workers, often interfering with their work. When the tradesperson mentions the bothersome man to people who work at the mansion, it soon becomes clear that the meddlesome observer is none other than the original owner of the home—Frederick Pabst.

He appears to be carefully overseeing the upkeep of his magnificent home even after his death.

Could Captain Pabst still haunt the halls of his beautiful mansion? The answer to this eerie mystery is something best decided while exploring this historic building for yourself. If you get a chance to take a tour of the historic Pabst Mansion, keep an eye open for Captain Pabst. And if you do see him, perhaps let him know how beautiful his home is. I'm sure he'd appreciate that.

THE ENDLESS ENCORE AT THE RIVERSIDE THEATER

It seems like every city has a haunted theater, and Milwaukee is no exception. People have flocked to this downtown landmark for almost one hundred years. When it opened in 1928, it was Milwaukee's favorite place to see vaudeville stars. Audiences filled the 2,460 seats to see the legendary Abbott and Costello and roar to the antics of the Three Stooges. Later it became a popular place to see movies and hear musicians who had a tour stop in Milwaukee. Today, people still come to the theater to see famous acts perform onstage and, if they're lucky, a spooky spirit as well.

The otherworldly spirits who have made the Riverside Theater their home are an active bunch of ghosts. Employees at the theater have had many eerie encounters with the paranormal inside the building, and they aren't shy about sharing their astonishing experiences!

One night, after a performance, an employee was locking up the theater. These late-night shifts were long and lonely, so he often brought along his dog for companionship. The man and his dog walked through the dark, empty hallways, locking doors and shutting off lights. Suddenly, the man heard a voice whisper the word "hey" directly into his ear. He froze in his tracks. No one else was in the hallway. Or even the building for that matter! He looked down at his dog and saw the poor creature trembling. When he saw how frightened the dog was, he knew he had not imagined hearing the voice!

The strange encounter terrified the dog so much he refused to take another step down the hallway. Eventually the man picked up the dog and carried him out of the theater. Some people believe that animals are more sensitive to supernatural experiences and can see and hear things that humans cannot. Was the dog so afraid because he could see the source of the mysterious whisper? Or was just hearing the otherworldly voice enough to paralyze the dog

with fear? Either way, the dog knew there was something scary in that hallway!

It is not known how many spirits still linger inside the Riverside Theater, but employees are certain one of ghosts is the spirit of a projectionist who worked there in the 1930s. The man died of a heart attack in the room where they operate the lighting at the theater. And his specter still lingers in the building where his life came to an unexpected end.

This ghost seems to have a good sense of humor and likes to amuse himself by teasing the current employees. More than one member of the staff has reported turning off the stage lights in the light room and then climbing down the many flights of stairs to get to stage level, only to find the stage lights have been turned back on! The confused employee will then again climb the stairs to reach the light room, only to find the stage lights are now shut off. The spirit of the room is a real prankster, as one round of this game with the lights is rarely enough for him. Eventually, the employee is able to get the stage lights to remain off, but only after rushing up and down the many flights of stairs countless times.

There have been so many unexplained, eerie events at the theater that a group of ghost hunters decided to do an investigation in 2011. The hunters made some spine-tingling discoveries. During their investigation, they

found cold spots all over the theater, which are believed to be a sign of a paranormal presence.

The team uncovered frightening activity in the theater's basement. They gathered reports from employees of a blue light hovering in the hallway of the basement. This mysterious light could be a spirit that was trying to make itself known to the staff. While deep inside the machine room, the ghost hunters recorded the sounds of a guttural, animal-like growl. Who—or what—made the disturbing sounds could not be identified, but they left everyone who heard them more than a bit rattled!

In a nearby room, close to the ice maker, employees reported the feeling of being touched or tapped by an unseen entity. No one knows if the spirit making physical contact with the living is the same one responsible for the scary sounds in the machine room, but all of this reported activity means only the bravest employees dare to go down to the basement.

However, it is not just the employees of the Riverside Theater who have had spine-tingling encounters with otherworldly entities. Visitors to the theater have caught the scent of cigar smoke from an unseen smoker. Others have reported sudden bursts of a strong floral perfume that seems to have no origin. If you don't find these puzzling odors from another realm frightening, maybe an apparition

might give you goosebumps! There have been reports of a ghostly man walking in the aisles of the theater when it is empty. This specter will occasionally choose one of the plush red theater seats and take a rest from his roaming.

Next time you are in the theater, take a look around you. If you see a man who looks a little hazy walking in the aisles, take a closer look. You may have just spied the mysterious specter. If you do, I just hope the spot next to you isn't open—and if it is, I hope he doesn't feel like having a seat . . .

NEXT AT BAT: THE PFISTER GHOST

The most famously haunted building in Milwaukee is the Pfister Hotel. Year after year, it tops the lists of Wisconsin's creepiest, spookiest places. There are many reports of a ghost haunting the Pfister Hotel. And one of the reasons the Pfister Ghost has become so well known is because a number of Major League Baseball players claimed to have seen it during a stay at the luxury hotel.

So who is the Pfister Ghost? Most people think the spirit who haunts the halls is Charles Pfister. Guido Pfister dreamed of building the finest hotel in the land. Sadly, Guido died before he had the chance to do that. But his son, Charles, saw that his father's dream became a reality. And he was in charge of the hotel from the day it opened in 1893 until he died in 1927. Charles loved the hotel, and many people believe he is still watching over the Pfister from the afterlife.

If you are hoping to have a spooky experience at the hotel, you are in luck! It is not just baseball players who have eerie interactions with Charles Pfister; many guests have reported seeing him. There have been reports of the portly and clean-shaven ghost of Pfister wandering through the original portion of the hotel. Floors one through seven existed in Pfister's lifetime. He is not known to appear in the newer portion of the building. Do you want to catch a glimpse of Charles Pfister? You might want to try going to the ballroom. It is said the well-dressed apparition of the former owner sometimes lingers there.

You might want to meet Mr. Pfister, but plenty of baseball players quake in their cleats at the thought of encountering him. Here are just a few of the stories baseball players have shared about their creepy stays in the hotel when they have been in town to play the Milwaukee Brewers.

In 2018, St. Louis Cardinals pitcher Carlos Martinez said he saw a ghost in his hotel room. The apparition shook him up so much that he jumped onto Instagram in the middle of the night to share his paranormal experience. Martinez had a rough game the following day. He said his problems on the field that day were caused by the heebie-jeebies from his spooky late-night encounter.

Anaheim Angels first baseman Ji-Man Choi also had a memorable stay at the hotel. In 2016, he reported that a misty spirit hovered over his bed as he was trying to fall asleep. Choi is not the only Angel who had a strange experience in the hotel. Pitcher C.J. Wilson recalled a time when he had an electrical disturbance in his room. It began with the light bulb in a bedside lamp flickering. Within moments, the lamp turned off. A minute later, his television turned off. He sat for a moment, wondering if there was a supernatural entity in the room.

Eerily, as soon as the thought crossed his mind, the lamp and the television turned back on. Then the overhead light by the doorway of the room shut itself off. He took a deep breath, and then he heard a strange scratching sound that seemed to come from INSIDE the wall! The unexplained noises continued through the night. As the hours ticked by, Wilson grew more convinced something otherworldly was in that room with him!

And it seems the Pfister Ghost has an ear for music. In 2009, Giants third baseman Pablo Sandoval was taking a shower in his room when his iPod suddenly turned itself on and

started to play a song. Cincinnati Reds second baseman Brandon Phillips was relaxing in his room when the radio began to play. He turned the radio off and headed into the shower. From behind the shower curtain, he heard the radio switch on again! It seems the ghost is determined to play some tunes when stopping in to check on the players.

Perhaps the most peculiar story to come from a baseball player who stayed at the hotel is the one told by Bryce Harper, who was the right fielder for the Washington Nationals at the time. Before he went to sleep, he put his clothes for the next day on the bench that was at the foot of his bed. When Harper woke up the next morning, his clothes were on the floor, and the bench had been moved to the other side of the room! No one else was in his room that night. Harper could not find an explanation for how the heavy bench moved across the room by itself without making a sound! The experience unnerved him so much that he packed his belongings and went to the hotel's front desk. There he demanded a new room—and one on a different floor!

So many players have had spooky experiences at the Pfister that some actually refuse to stay at the hotel. Others will stay at the hotel, but only if they share a room with another player. And at least one player has admitted that when he stays at the Pfister, he sleeps with a bat in his bed for protection.

There are few teams in the National League who haven't had at least one player claim to have a paranormal experience in the hotel. Except, of course, the Milwaukee Brewers. It seems as if the Pfister Ghost is always rooting for the home team. It is well known that Brewers who stay at the hotel for home games are said to have peaceful—and very uneventful—nights! Teams in town to play against the home team? Well, they don't sleep quite as soundly!

The next time you are at the Pfister Hotel, be on the lookout for Charles. If you see him, be sure to let him know that Bernie Brewer sent you!

THE FRIGHTFUL FIREHOUSE

How do the departed react when their final resting place turns out to be not so final after all? For the spirits of those entombed at the former Fairview Mausoleum, the shock of having their bodies moved might have made them restless. A mausoleum is a building where the dead, inside of a coffin, are sealed into a wall of the building. Think of it as being buried above ground.

In 1912, the Fairview Mausoleum was built on the west side of Milwaukee. The black stone building held the remains of 999 of the city's dearly departed. Even when it was brand new, it was a scary-looking building. Especially on the days when smoke billowed from the crematorium. As years passed, people stopped taking care of the property. The building grew shabby. The lawn was overgrown. The concrete walkways began to crumble, and weeds grew in the cracks. Wind and rain howled through shattered windows that had been broken by vandals. Neighborhood children believed the decrepit building was haunted. They were so

frightened of the place that they would avoid walking on the mausoleum's side of the street.

By 1996, the building was in such bad shape that the city decided to tear it down. The remains of the 999 people inside the mausoleum were relocated to the Graceland Cemetery. The process took almost a year, but eventually, all of the departed were laid to rest in Section Eleven of the sprawling graveyard grounds. This time, rather than being entombed above ground, as they had been for decades, they were buried in the ground.

It may have been moving the deceased that roused their spirits. Or maybe it was placing their remains in a hole in the earth and covering them with shovelfuls of dirt, contrary to their final wishes. Either way, the spirits seemed to be quite comfortable and peaceful where the Fairview Mausoleum had been, and so it appears they decided to linger there even after the mausoleum was gone.

The city immediately started building a new firehouse on the grounds of the former mausoleum. Engine House 35 was completed in 1998. This modern building doesn't look like

the kind of place where restless spirits would dwell. But the building has so many reports of paranormal activity that the firefighters have nicknamed it the "Crypt Keeper."

Firefighters on the day and night shifts have reported hearing the sounds of footsteps

coming from vacant hallways of the engine house. Mischievous spirits have also been known to throw pots and pans in the empty kitchen. Bolder spirits in the house have interacted with the firefighters.

Two firefighters shared an unnerving event that happened while they were relaxing in the firehouse. The pair were sitting on either side of a floor lamp when they witnessed the plug of the lamp fly out of the outlet in the wall. The room was instantly plunged into darkness. Neither of the witnesses could explain how the plug was forcefully pulled from outlet without being touched.

Even eerier is the story told by a firefighter who was sleeping in the basement of the engine house. He was startled awake from a deep sleep to the feeling of being violently held down. He wrestled with the unseen entity in an attempt to sit up in bed. It was a struggle, but the strong fireman was eventually able to free himself from the grasp of the invisible intruder. The next morning, he discovered bruises on his torso in the exact places the unknown force pinned him onto the mattress.

Are these hair-raising happenings the result of building the firehouse on grounds that were meant to be the final resting place for almost one thousand people? If so, the identities of the spirits responsible for most of the supernatural activities remain a mystery. But not all of the otherworldly beings in the firehouse are anonymous.

There are some who believe they know the identity of one of the ghosts that haunt the firehouse: Captain Edward Gifford Crosby. The Crosby family was prominent in Milwaukee. Captain Crosby owned a transportation company. He was married to Catherine, and together they had a son named Fred and a daughter named Harriette.

Crosby, along with his wife and daughter, were first-class passengers on the maiden voyage of the RMS *Titanic* when it sank in 1912. His family was able to scramble into a lifeboat, but Crosby drowned in the icy waters of the Atlantic Ocean. His body was later recovered and returned to Milwaukee. His family cremated him and had his ashes placed inside the mausoleum. When his wife and, later, his

daughter died, their bodies were placed next to his in the mausoleum.

Since the station has opened, there have been a number of reports of the bathroom water faucet turning on by itself in the middle of the night. When this occurs, the tap is always fully opened, and the water is frigidly cold. Some think this strange occurrence is Crosby, who died in icy water, trying to communicate with the living inside the firehouse.

What do you think? Are the torrents of icy water that flow from the tap meant to represent the bitterly cold ocean water that flooded the ill-fated *Titanic*? Does all of this cold water point to the presence Captain Crosby in the engine house? This next encounter might help to convince you.

Another night shift firefighter awoke in the early-morning hours to see an apparition next to his bed. The spirit—dressed in a bowler hat, vest, and woolen pants—disappeared without a trace when the fireman turned to look at him more closely. Strange, right? It gets even stranger when you find out that when Crosby's body was recovered from the ocean, he was found wearing a green tweed suit that included a vest! Crosby was found hatless, but bowler hats were a popular fashion on the boat, so it is possible Crosby was wearing a hat when the ship sank, and it was lost in the waves.

Could all this activity be just a way for the spirits to let everyone know they are still here, even if their remains are not? No one can be sure, but one thing seems certain: there is definitely something unusual happening at Engine House 35.

Enter this wild wood and view the haunts of nature

Entrance to Grant Park's Seven Bridges Trail

CHAPTER 2

Petrifying Parks

Milwaukee County is home to more than 140 public parks. These parks are great places to get some fresh air and enjoy nature. Nothing strange or scary every happens in a park, right?

Well, in Milwaukee, there are a few parks that might make you change your mind about that! There is definitely something spooky lurking in these popular gathering places. The next time you are in the park and you hear something rustling in the bushes, you might want to investigate. It could be a squirrel or a rabbit, but it just might be something spine-chillingly creepy.

On second thought, don't look, just run!

THE MYSTERY OF THE LAKE PARK GHOSTS

There are few hauntings as mysterious as the one surrounding Lake Park. Ask any Milwaukeean to direct you to a haunted location around town, and Lake Park's Lions Bridge is certain to be one of the first places they'll mention.

There are some people who go to the famous park just to seek out the ghosts rumored to lurk there. When visitors arrive at the bridge, they encounter the stern stone faces of the massive lion statues that stand guard over the pathway. An ominous feeling of dread washes over them as they stare into the lion's unblinking eyes. As these brave ghost hunters walk past the lions, some claim to feel the icy tingle of a supernatural presence on the bridge. Even on hot summer days, visitors have reported experiencing cold spots on the bridge. As already mentioned, many people believe ghosts often make themselves known by dropping the temperature in a specific area.

In addition to the eerie cold spots, sometimes people report hearing the faint sounds of children's laughter around the bridge when there aren't any children nearby. It wouldn't be strange to hear kids playing in a park, but those who have heard the sound insist it is not the joyful laughter of kids at play. They describe a sinister laughter that sent chills down their spines and warned them that something otherworldly was nearby. Many think these unseen ghosts are guarding the bridge—and it seems to be working! These

spirits keep all but the very brave from visiting the popular area alone.

These creepy encounters puzzle visitors. There was never a tragedy involving the death of a group of children in Lake Park. Why these spirits are in the park is a mystery to ghost seekers—that is, unless you consider that Lake Park was built on mounds built by Indigenous people a very long time ago.

Before the land was a park, it was home to people who belonged to a group called the Mid-Woodland Culture. These Native people lived in the area more than two thousand years ago. Not a lot is known about these people, but

we do know the park was the place where they practiced sacred rituals and buried their dead in special mounds.

These mounds are huge piles of dirt that are often sculpted into the shapes of animals. Some of the mounds are as big as an airplane! These mounds are basically a tomb. The Mid-Woodland people would bury their dead in the mounds, and they would also bury objects they thought the dead would need in the afterlife. The area used to have a lot of these tombs, but they were destroyed when the park was built. Today, only one of these ancient mounds remains.

Some people think the ghosts in the park are the spirits of the people whose final resting place was destroyed. Are these ghostly children protecting an area sacred to them? Or are they angry with the living for disturbing the sacred mounds? What do you think?

We'll probably never know who these spirits are, or why they're here, but it doesn't seem likely that they are leaving anytime soon. Do you want to experience theses strange happenings for yourself? Muster up the courage to walk past the stone lions and onto the bridge—if you dare!

GHASTLY GHOSTS OF GRANT PARK

When entering Grant Park's Seven Bridges Trail, walkers are greeted by a sign that reads, "Enter this wild wood and view the haunts of nature." If the legends are to be believed, far more than nature haunts these mystical trails. Once the sun sets, the spirits of those long dead, but not gone, make themselves known.

The park was created in 1900. A few decades later, during the Great Depression, unemployed Milwaukeeans were hired to make the park bigger and better. They built the park's stone paths and staircases. Most importantly, they constructed the seven bridges along the popular two-mile trail. Even though it is in the city, the park on the shore of Lake Michigan feels far away from the hustle and bustle of busy streets that surround the park. If you walk on the forest trail in the daytime, you will see joggers and families strolling with baby carriages. But at night, the trail belongs to the spirits that have made Seven Bridges Trail their home.

The many stories of strange phenomenon on the dark trails lure in those hoping to have a supernatural experience. Generations of brave (or foolish—you decide!) ghost hunters have crept along the well-traveled trails on the blackest of nights, seeking an encounter with "the other side." A number of these seekers have reported seeing unexplained colored lights dancing in the woods. The sudden appearance of the strange lights never fails to send a chill down the spines of those who have witnessed them. And the source of those lights, and what they mean, are still a mystery waiting to be solved.

Even more frightening are the hair-raising encounters ghost hunters have had on the main bridge of the trail. Many a tale has been told of tragic deaths in the ravine below the bridge. It is believed the spirits of some of those unfortunate people still linger near the spot where they took their last breaths.

A number of nighttime walkers have reported seeing a misty apparition on the first bridge on the trail. This blurry form is sometimes known to rise from under the bridge and join the shocked ghost hunters. In a few instances, the gauzy ghost, without warning, appeared RIGHT next to the ghost hunters. The jolt of fear felt by the stunned hunters who have had the experience stops them in their tracks. With knees knocking, they run off the bridge, unwilling to take another step into the park.

Ghost hunters who have the courage to move beyond the bridge claim there are even more frights waiting along the wooded trails. The brave ones who make it to the stone bench along the path report hearing terrified screams from deep inside the empty woods. Searches through the woods for a person in distress are always unsuccessful. No one is there. At least no one who can be seen. Could it be the spirit

of someone whose life ended in the woods, warning the walkers of danger that lies ahead?

Those on a search for the supernatural will sometimes dare to seek spirits on an unpaved portion of the trail near the beach. It is there they have encountered the specter of a woman in great distress. The woman glows in the unlit park. She is wearing a long white gown that flutters in the wind, even on calm nights. She is silent, but those who have seen her face say it looks like she is crying. This ghostly woman paces the area as if searching for something that she will never find. It is believed this luminous lady is the mother of two young boys who drowned long ago in Lake Michigan's cold depths. There she remains, forever tormented by the terrible loss of her children.

If all of that isn't enough to send a shiver down your spine, listen to what happened to a few gutsy ghost hunters who kept walking down the dark trail, despite the specters and ghostly screams they encountered. As those adventurous few continued on the unlit path, they heard footsteps stomping through the forest undergrowth and the sounds of heavy breathing. They shined their flashlights into the woods but saw nothing. As they continued to search for the source of the sound, the footsteps grew nearer, and the breathing began thundering in their ears. In a flash, the sounds quickly passed over the hunters, leaving behind nothing but a feeling of fear and dread in its wake.

What do you think of these nighttime ghost hunts on the Seven Bridges Trail in Grant Park? For me, not even a triple-dog dare could convince me to step into those woods at night! I prefer the haunts of nature over these scary stories of specters that are supposed to haunt these woods. How about you?

THE PROTECTIVE MOTHER

People love visiting Whitnall Park! At 627 acres, it is the largest of the Milwaukee County Parks. This park provides fun activities for everyone. In addition to the playgrounds and picnic sites most parks have, Whitnall Park also has a golf course, a nature center, and botanical gardens. Oh, and did I mention it has its very own ghost? Yep, it sure does!

Whitnall's spectacular specter is elusive, but she IS there. If you seek out this mysterious ghost, you can find her by following the river until you reach the Whitnall Pond. Once you

are there, walk over to the waterfall on the northern end of the pond. As you make your way along the path, notice the temperature of the air as you get nearer to the waterfall. You might find the air gets colder. If it does, stay alert. That cold air could signal you are in the presence the spirit that has lingered in the area for longer than anyone can remember.

The ghost is a pale, wispy figure in white. She hovers, rather than walks, because she does not have any feet. When she appears, people report they can also hear the sound of a baby crying. The cries of a wailing infant can be

heard above the din of the waterfall, but a child has never been seen. The spirit is believed to be a mother whose baby is in distress.

You might think that a ghost that stays so well hidden would flee when she is spotted. In fact, she does the opposite. Her footless form floats towards the park visitors who see her. But be on your guard. She doesn't want you to get closer to her. She wants to scare you away from the area!

As her hazy figure gets closer to you—her unwanted guest—she can sometimes be heard calling out. Her ghostly voice warns intruders to stay away and to leave her baby alone. As she speaks, park visitors feel the hair rise on the backs of their necks. After she issues her warning, she then disappears into the brush, seemingly to tend to the unseen baby still crying in the distance. The frightening encounters leave those who see her shaken—and puzzled.

Who is this protective mother caring for her crying baby? Why is her spirit tied to this area? Is she reliving events that happened long ago when the area was still farmland? These are questions to ask yourself as you stroll around the riverway in the park. One can only guess what answers you might find when you reach the roar of the waterfall. Well, that is if you dare to seek out this ghostly mother.

Grave at La Belle Cemetery

CHAPTER 3

Ghosts in the Graveyard

Have you ever played Ghost in the Graveyard? It's a spooky nighttime game for three or more people that combines tag and hide-and-go-seek.

In this game, you choose one player to be "it." That player is the ghost. The ghost hides while everyone else closes their eyes and counts "one o'clock, two o'clock, three o'clock," until they get to midnight. When the group yells midnight, they run in search of the ghost. When players spot the ghost, they shout, "Ghost in the graveyard! Run, run, run!" Then all players attempt to get safely home before the ghost catches them. The ghost begins to chase the players. If the ghost tags someone, that person becomes a ghost in the next round.

Sounds fun, right? Visiting these graveyards is a bit like playing that game. Except these ghosts aren't hiding. And they aren't playing a game. They are real, and they still linger in the cemeteries that should have been their final resting places. If only they would rest!

Read on, if you dare!

The Two Spooky Specters of Tabernacle Cemetery

After someone dies, what might keep their spirit connected to our world? No one can say for sure, but the ghosts that hang around Tabernacle Cemetery in Delafield might give us some clues. It appears that two spirits have made this lonely, rural graveyard, established in 1842, their home. One ghost is young and the other is old, and both died very near their final resting places. But, if you believe the stories, theses spirits aren't doing much resting!

The younger ghost is thought to be the first person buried in the graveyard. He was

a farm boy who tragically died in an accident on a nearby farm. He met his untimely end inside the barn that overlooked the area that became the cemetery. The farmer who owned the barn was so sad over the sudden death of the farmhand that nothing could comfort him. Day after day, the farmer would look across the field at the boy's grave. He couldn't eat. He couldn't sleep. All he could do was mourn the loss of the boy.

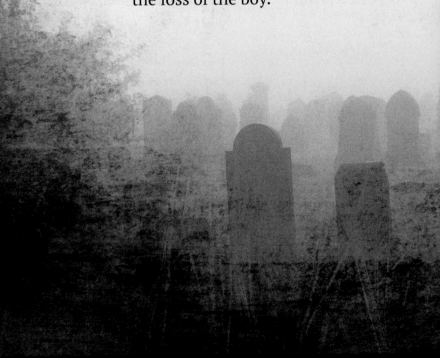

The farmer did not think a tombstone was big enough to honor the memory of the young boy. He wanted the boy to be remembered by something bigger than a monument or a statue, so he turned to the biggest thing he could think of: his barn. The grieving farmer grabbed a can of paint, a brush, and a ladder, then spent the rest of the day painting the boy's name on the side of his barn in the largest letters he could manage. When he was done, the boy's name could be seen from a very long way away.

Before long, the story of the farmer's memorial to the boy spread to nearby towns. People would drive their horse-drawn carriages along the dusty road that passed the barn to stop and take in the boy's name in giant letters. They could sense the farmer's pain, and it broke their hearts.

Not long after the boy's name was painted on the barn, mysterious lights began to appear in the graveyard. This was in the days before electricity. Those who saw the lights shine in the dark night were shocked by how bright they were. People had seen a candle flickering at night, and the light from an oil lantern, but they had never, ever seen lights that were as bright as the ones that shone from the new cemetery. These otherworldly white lights have twinkled in the twilight of the quiet cemetery ever since—for over 150 years!

Those who have witnessed this nighttime light show feel certain the young farmhand is the source of these eerie lights. Many people believe it is farmer's tribute to the farmhand's death that keeps the boy's spirit connected to the small cemetery. Is the boy using the lights to let people know he is okay?

The older spirit that calls the Tabernacle Cemetery home is a short, stout, middle-aged

man. He is often seen lingering near the cemetery sign on Bryn Drive. It is believed the man died in a car accident along that stretch of road. He appears without warning on the side of the road—and disappears just as quickly. Does his spirit haunt this area to warn drivers of danger on the dark and winding remote road? Or is his presence meant to scare drivers into an accident of their own? No one knows why he shows himself to drivers, but all who have seen him say it was a spine-tingling and unnerving encounter they will never forget.

Today, the Tabernacle Cemetery grounds are closed to visitors—at least to the ones that are still living. If you drive by the gated grounds at night, be on the lookout for signs of bright lights peeking through the trees. They could be a sign of the farm boy's restless spirit. And as your car approaches the cemetery sign, you just might get the chance to see the spirit of the middle-aged man jump out to say hello!

THE SPIRIT OF THE STONE GIRL

A stone statue can't come to life. Or can it? That is the question that visitors to La Belle Cemetery have been asking for years. Legend has it that the cemetery is a hotbed of paranormal happenings. The source of this unearthly activity appears to be the final resting place of a family who were early residents of Oconomowoc. The spot is marked by a life-sized stone statue of a young girl.

The story is often told that at dusk, the shimmering spirit of a girl will appear in front of this stone statue. No one knows just who this otherworldly being is. Some people think it is the spirit of the girl who was the model for the statue. Some people think it is the spirit of a girl buried somewhere else in the graveyard. Who she is remains a mystery, but people are sure she is somehow connected to the eerie statue.

Those who have seen the spooky sight say if you dare to approach this glowing ghost, she will flee in the direction of Fowler Lake. When she gets to the shore, she throws herself into

the water, disappears under the surface, and is not seen again. At least not that night. But this same strange scene has been repeated again and again for years.

As you can imagine, lots of people come to the cemetery in hopes of seeing this famous ghost. Over the years, curious visitors have left small gifts for the statue at the grave site. Some bring fresh flowers to place on top of the stone flowers the statue holds in her arms. Others leave coins or trinkets in the statue's cupped hands. It is said that bad luck will come to anyone who dares to take something that has been left for the statue. To be on the safe side, I'd leave the stone girl's gift alone if I were you. But it's just a statue. It can't really do anything to you. Right?

Muirdale Santatorium

CHAPTER 4

The Spooky Suburbs

Some people believe Wisconsin is the most haunted state in the country. A professor from the University of Wisconsin, Robert E. Gard, once famously said that "Wisconsin contains more ghosts per square mile than any other state in the nation." If that is true, you know ghosts aren't just in the big cities. Milwaukee is great, but the suburbs have plenty of terrifying tales, too.

Here are just a few stories from the suburbs that will send a tingle up your spine.

SOMETHING STRANGE AT
THE STAGECOACH INN

People come from all over to tour the Dousman
Stagecoach Inn Museum in Brookfield. The inn
was built in 1842, six years before Wisconsin
became a state. It was a place for people to stop
and rest as they made the long journey from
Milwaukee to the frontier towns springing up
in the western part of the state. At the roadside
inn, weary travelers could rest their horses and
get a home-cooked meal and a clean bed for
the night. It wasn't a home away from home,
but it was as close as you could get while on
the road. And some believe there are guests
who enjoyed their stay at the inn so much that
they never checked out!

No one knows who the mysterious spirits
are that continue to roam through the
three-story wooden building. But if you believe
the reports, they seem to be friendly. A woman

who worked at the museum tells the story of a ghost who gave her a helping hand while she was alone in the building. She had her arms full of packages when she came upon a closed door. She groaned and looked for a spot to drop her packages so she could open the door. Suddenly, the doorknob turned and the door creaked opened, seemingly by itself.

After putting the packages down in another room, she examined the doorknob, which seemed to be working correctly. How did the door suddenly open?

Could this be the same helpful spirit who steadied an employee when she nearly fell while hanging decorations in the museum? The woman stood on a chair and strained to tape a streamer to a place on the wall that was just beyond her reach. She felt the chair wobble beneath her, and she began to lose her balance. Just before she expected to slip off the chair, she felt a hand steady her. When she regained her composure, she turned around to thank the kind person who helped her avoid a painful tumble. It was then she realized she was in the room alone. She slowly climbed down from the chair, shaken and wondering who—or what—had come to her aid.

All of these good deeds might just be a bit exhausting for this helpful ghost, and he or she sometimes needs a break. On more than one occasion, groups touring the building have noticed the rocking chair in the second floor master bedroom moving on its own. Surprised visitors watch as the empty chair gently creaks back and forth on the worn wooden floor.

We don't know if the helpful ghost and the spirit that uses the rocking chair are one and the same. But it seems certain there are ghostly guests at the inn who have no plans to check out anytime soon. If you visit the museum to see a glimpse of the past, be sure to stay alert. You never know who you might meet. It just might be one of the spirits who decided to extend their stay FOREVER!

Gentlemen, Start Your Engines

Fitzsimmons Road, Oak Creek's infamous "road to nowhere," has been closed to traffic for more than twenty years. But that has not stopped visitors, both living and dead, from flocking to this eerie stretch of road.

In the 1950s and 1960s, this out-of-the-way, dead-end road was used as a drag racing strip by adventurous local teens. A typical race night would find the popular strip lined with cheering crowds illuminated only by the headlights of the rowdy racers. Cars would tear down the strip, their engines revving and tires squealing on the concrete. The races abruptly ended where the pavement stopped on the dead-end road . . . or, at least, they should have.

At the end of the road is a wooden barricade. Just beyond the barricade is a cliff that hovers two hundred feet above Lake Michigan. If a car could not stop and drove past the barrier, it made an eighteen-story drop into the water! A fall like that would mean certain death to anyone in the car. The wooden barriers did little to stop the two tons of racing steel barreling down Fitzsimmons Road. Legend has it that a number of racers, unable to stop at the barricades, careened off the jagged cliff and plunged to their watery graves at the bottom of the lake.

It has been long believed that unlucky racers, some who drowned in the lake, others who died in fiery crashes, still linger on this lonely road. People claim to see mysterious headlights racing down the road. And these headlights do not stop at the end of the road. The glowing lights speed past the barricades and off the cliff, only to disappear under Lake Michigan's cold waves. A number of people have reported seeing the apparition of one of those racers whose brakes failed as he reached the end of the road. The glowing white figure

of this young man appears on the rocky shores of the lake. The apparition shines in the darkness as he scales the cliff on his way back to Fitzsimmons Road.

These days, cars are no longer able to access this closed part of Fitzsimmons Road, but thrill-seekers are still drawn to the spot, eager to see for themselves the otherworldly traces of these dangerous races. Ghost hunters, traveling on foot, claim to hear sounds of engines revving, sometimes joined by the sounds of cars crashing and terror-filled screams. These spirits that remain, pulled from life so suddenly, appear to be forever trapped in the tragic night of their final race. Are you one of the curious? Would you dare to walk along the deserted road, lit only by moonlight, to search for the source of these otherworldly happenings? There is only one way to find out. You go first, I'll wait for you.

A COUGH IN THE DARK

The Muirdale Santatorium was built in 1915 to treat people with tuberculous. This highly contagious, airborne disease caused a chronic cough, fever, rapid weight loss, and night sweats. Patients were plagued with mucous-filled lungs—the thick, white phlegm inside the lungs caused bone-rattling coughs and earned the disease the terrifying name the "White Plague." The constant coughing damaged the patient's airways, making it very common for patients to cough up blood. It was common in those days to cough into a handkerchief to prevent the spread of germs. A blood-splattered handkerchief was the telltale sign that someone had caught the dreaded disease.

In the early 1900s, most of the medicines we have today had not yet been invented, so there was little that could be done to help those who had contracted tuberculosis. About half the people who caught the disease died. At the turn of the century, 450 Americans died from the disease every day. Muirdale Santatorium closed in 1978 after treating tens of thousands of tuberculous patients. Sadly, many of those patients did not leave the sanitorium alive.

The redbrick building is still standing today. It is now the Technology Innovation Center, and it is home to more than forty small businesses. Both inside and outside, the appearance of the building has changed little since it was used to care for the sick. The medical equipment has been removed from the building, but most things still look the same. Maybe it is those familiar interiors that keep spirits connected to the structure. Whatever

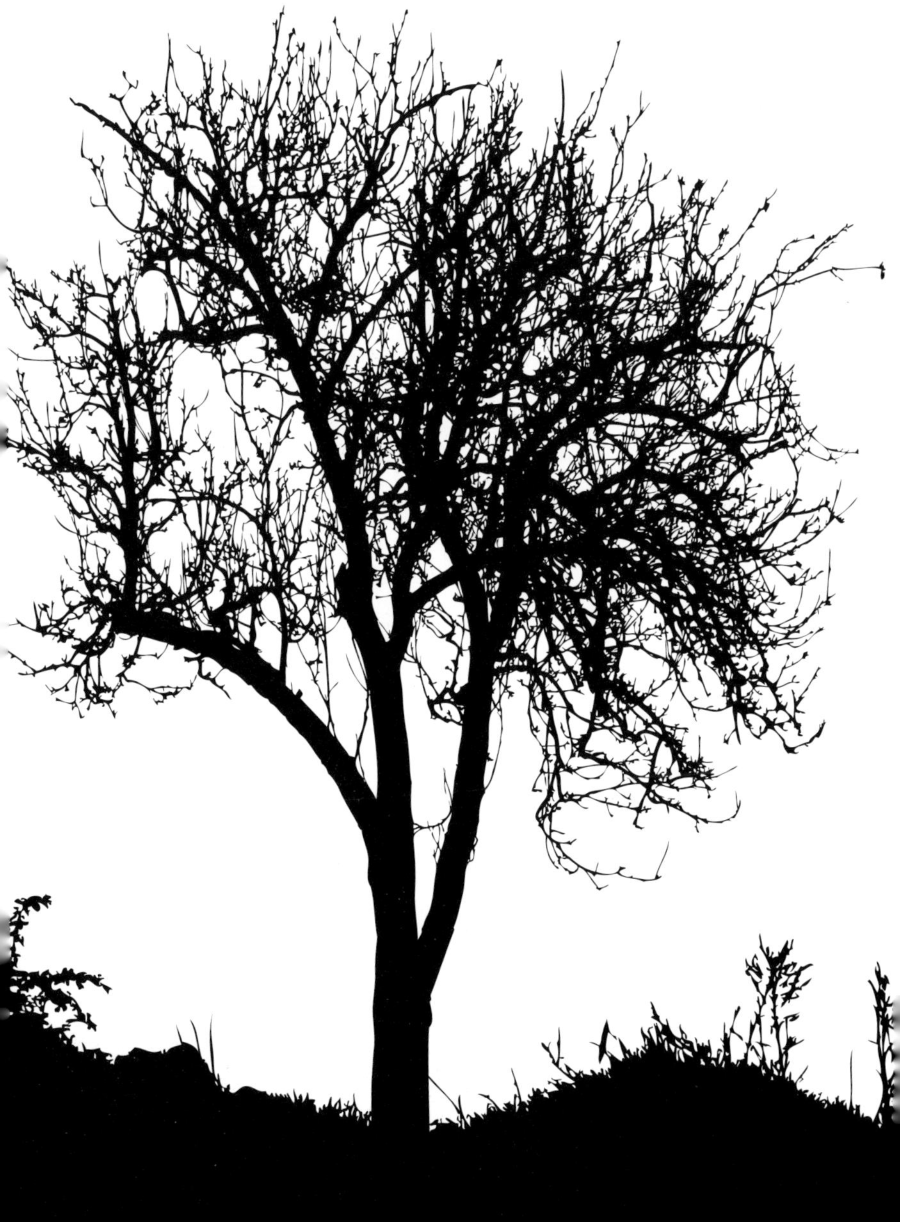

the reason, this building in Research Park is among the most haunted in Milwaukee.

Paranormal activity has been reported and ghostly apparitions have been spotted on every floor of the building. Many of these active spirits are former patients of the sanitorium, but there are still a few nurses whose final shifts have continued into the afterlife. The sounds of a deep, hacking cough echo in the empty hallways throughout the building. When these coughing fits are heard, the source of these noises cannot be found.

Those who work in the building have witnessed the shocking sight of long-dead patients roaming the halls of the former sanitorium in their hospital gowns. Many of the former treatment rooms are now offices. More than one visitor to the building has told of the heart-pounding experience of walking into an empty office only to find ghostly figures waiting to be seen by a doctor.

The fifth floor of the building seems to be particularly active. Spirits have been both seen and heard, and it is not uncommon for heavy doors to suddenly be slammed shut by an unseen hand.

One former employee tells of a spine-tingling encounter with an apparition while he was working late into the evening and alone on the fifth floor. He took his dinner into what he *thought* would be an empty meeting room. He walked through the doorway of the room, eager to dig into his food. He looked up and found himself face-to-face with a ghostly figure in a nurse's uniform. He was so startled it took him a few moments to believe what his eyes saw. Once he realized he was in the same room with a ghost, he ran down the hallway as fast as his legs could carry him. The ghostly nurse did not follow him, but the encounter scared him enough to make sure he never worked alone on that floor again!

A building with this many active spirits is bound to attract ghost hunters. Many nighttime visitors to the grounds have claimed to see a chilling sight when they look up to the windows on the fifth floor. Staring back at them are the faces of former patients! Their hollow eyes gaze out from their pale faces into the night.

The spirits seem to be most active at night, but they do not rest after the sun rises. Daytime visitors often report seeing something move out of the corner of their eye. A person or a shadow? They aren't sure. When they turn their heads to see what moved, they find nothing is there. In the hallways, people have experienced the feeling that someone is standing near them. Whatever that presence is, it cannot be seen. Those who spend a lot of time in the Technology Innovation Center have the feeling they are never truly alone in the building, even when they are in empty rooms. At least, the rooms APPEAR to be empty!

Can you imagine working at the Technology Innovation Center? It might be a little creepy, but at least you'll always have someone to each your lunch with, even if you are the only one there!

THE BRAY ROAD MYSTERY

It is a werewolf? Could it just be a stray dog? Or is it something else entirely? That is the mystery at the heart of the story of the Beast of Bray Road. On a lonely stretch of rural road in Elkhorn, Wisconsin, lurks a mysterious creature that has astonished all those who have seen it. And there are dozens who have claimed to encounter the mysterious creature.

What does this creature look like? No one can say for certain. Interestingly, when people who have seen the beast describe the animal, none of the descriptions of this strange creature seem to match the details given by other witnesses. While the details might not be identical, everyone who has seen it says the creature will stand on its hind legs, and when it does, it is as tall as a human adult!

Some people recount that the creature they saw has a shaggy coat of long, dark hair. Others recall that its fur was streaked with silver or gray. Many who have seen the animal describe its head as having a long muzzle and pointed ears, similar to the head of a German shepherd. But some who have seen the animal disagree. They think it looks more like an ape than a dog. While people don't agree on what the beast looks like, there IS one thing each witness has described. Each person who has seen the animal has mentioned its eyes. They remember the intense, penetrating stare from the animal's cold, yellow eyes. That chilling stare shook each witness down to their core.

The first known sighting of the Beast of Bray Road was in 1936. It was spotted by a nighttime security guard at the rural, isolated campus of St. Coletta's School. While the guard patrolled the grounds after midnight, he encountered a strange creature clawing the ground. As the guard moved closer to try

to identify the animal, the mysterious creature crawled towards him. As it crept nearer to the guard, the beast suddenly stood on its hind legs. Unbelievably, the creature appeared to be more than six feet tall!

The stunned man was frozen in place. The guard noticed that the animal was covered in dark hair and smelled strongly of rotting flesh. The creature turned to the man and stared right into his eyes. The animal held the man's gaze and would not turn away. While the beast's eyes were locked on the guard's face, the creature began to snarl. The terrified man described the sound as a deep, unearthly growl. Trembling, the guard slowly walked away from the animal. With every step he took, he prayed the unknown animal would leave him alone. When telling this story, the guard remembers that he felt the beast's eyes boring into his back.

While the frightened guard never saw the beast again, many others have. During the late 1980s and through to the early 1990s, a number of people reported seeing the mysterious beast. The reports of the strange animal caught the attention of writer Linda Godfrey. Linda lived near the road where the beast was spotted. She decided to investigate the sightings and write about what people saw lurking in the dark in Elkhorn.

Linda's stories appeared in the local paper. They became so popular that before long, people all over the world wanted to know more about the mysterious animal spotted prowling around Bray Road. When Linda interviewed the people who saw the animal, she found that people were surprised by its human characteristics. They also said the animal was fast. People told of its panther-like run as it fled from the unexpected human encounters.

Frighteningly, the animal was also said to have big and powerful claws. Several witnesses reported that the animal dug into the side of their cars with its sharp claws. Yes! The animal was able to slice into metal with its claws! Pretty scary stuff!

Some of the people Linda interviewed were so frightened by what they saw that they were convinced the being must be otherworldly. They could not believe something so terrifying was produced by nature!

After the Bray Road Beast sightings made world news, people were determined to find out what it was that people were seeing on this lonesome stretch of road. Lots of

people scoffed at the idea that a mysterious, dangerous creature was roaming through Elkhorn. They came to the town to try to prove the animal did not exist. Despite their best efforts, the nonbelievers have never proven that the creature seen by witnesses was a wolf, bear, stray dog, or any other known animal. The mystery continues to this day.

So, the question you need to ask yourself is, are you ready to search Bray Road for the mysterious beast? If so, I hope you find it before it finds you!

Well, you've just been introduced to some of Milwaukee's most famous and spookiest ghosts. What do you think? Are these ghosts real? Is Milwaukee REALLY a haunted city? I hope you enjoyed these spook-tacular tales from

Brew City and that your spine was sufficiently tingled while reading the eerie tales.

Just one more thing, if you decide to go exploring in hopes of having your own ghostly encounter, watch out! You just might get more than you bargained for! Ghosts that seem a little creepy in the book just might be TERRIFYING in real life! Stay in groups, take notes, and always watch your back. You never know who—or what—might be right behind you!